Let's Get Ready for Martin Luther King Jr. Day

By Lloyd G. Douglas

Welcome Books™

Children's Press®
A Division of Scholastic Inc.
New York / Toronto / London / Auckland / Sydney
Mexico City / New Delhi / Hong Kong
Danbury, Connecticut

Photo Credits: Cover, pp. 5, 7, 11, 13, 15, 17, 19, 21 by Maura B. McConnell;
p. 9 © Flip Schulke/Corbis
Contributing Editor: Jennifer Silate
Book Design: Christopher Logan

Library of Congress Cataloging-in-Publication Data

Douglas, Lloyd G.
  Let's get ready for Martin Luther King Jr. Day / by Lloyd G. Douglas.
  p. cm. — (Celebrations)
  Includes index.
  Summary: A young boy and his class learn about and prepare for Martin
  Luther King Jr. Day.
  ISBN 0-516-24259-8 (lib. bdg.) — ISBN 0-516-24351-9 (pbk.)
  1. Martin Luther King Jr. Day—Juvenile literature. 2. King, Martin
  Luther, Jr., 1929-1968—Juvenile literature. [1. Martin Luther King
  Jr., Day. 2. King, Martin Luther, Jr., 1929-1968. 3. Holidays.] I.
  Title. II. Celebrations (Children's Press)

E185.97.K5 D66 2003
394.261—dc21

                                            2002007166

Contents

My name is Jake.

My class is getting ready for Martin Luther King Jr. Day.

This holiday is **celebrated** on Martin Luther King Jr.'s birthday.

My teacher tells us about Martin Luther King Jr.

She says that Martin Luther King Jr. helped many people.

Martin Luther King Jr.

by Tyrone Geter

SCHOLASTIC

Weather Tally

Sunny		
Partly Sunny		
Cloudy		
Windy		

Martin Luther King Jr. did not like that **African Americans** were not treated the same as others.

He wanted everyone to be kind to each other.

We are drawing **posters** of Martin Luther King Jr.

I draw him leading a **march**.

We **hang** up the posters of Martin Luther King Jr. in our **classroom**.

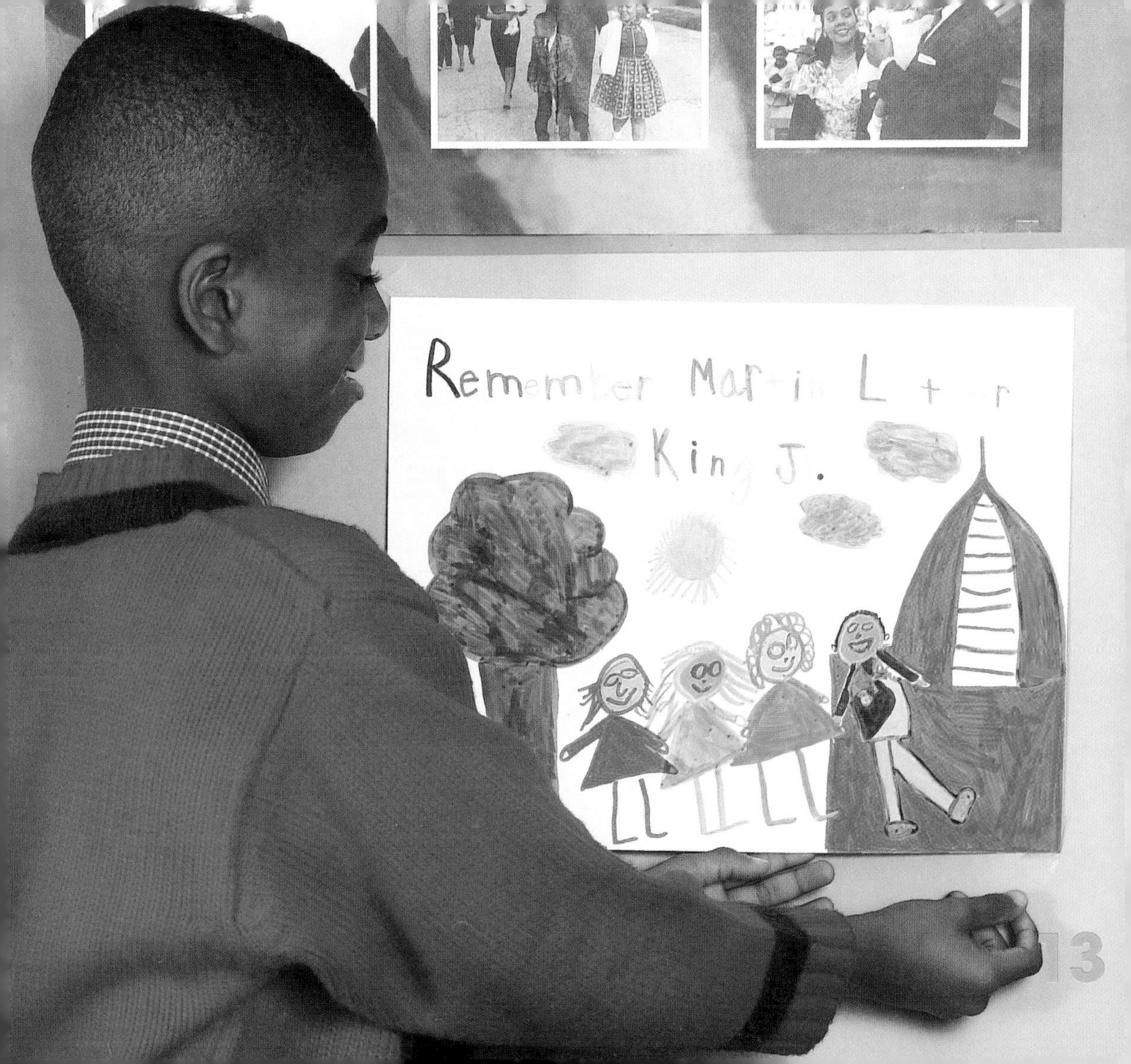
Remember
King J.

Today is Martin Luther King Jr. Day.

15

Mom and I celebrate by helping others today.

We are making food for our friend, Mrs. Smith.

Mom and I take the food to Mrs. Smith.

She is happy to get the food.

We will always remember Martin Luther King Jr.

New Words

African Americans (**af**-ruh-kuhn uh-**mer**-uh-kuhnz) people who were born in the United States or became U.S. citizens and can trace their ancestors back to Africa

celebrated (**sel**-uh-bray-tuhd) having done something enjoyable on a special occasion

classroom (**klass**-room) a room in a school in which classes take place

hang (**hang**) to fasten something somewhere

march (**march**) a large group of people walking together in order to let others know how they feel about something

posters (**poh**-sturz) large signs that often have pictures

To Find Out More

Books

Martin Luther King, Jr. Day
by Helen Frost
Pebble Books

Martin Luther King Jr. Day
by Mir Tamim Ansary
Heinemann Library

Web Site

Martin Luther King, Jr. Day
http://www.holidays.net/mlk/
Learn about Martin Luther King Jr. and send e-cards to your friends
and family on this Web site.

Index

About the Author

Lloyd G. Douglas is an editor and writer of children's books.

Reading Consultants

Kris Flynn, Coordinator, Small School District Literacy, The San Diego County Office of Education

Shelly Forys, Certified Reading Recovery Specialist, W.J. Zahnow Elementary School, Waterloo, IL

Sue McAdams, Former President of the North Texas Reading Council of the IRA, and Early Literacy Consultant, Dallas, TX